THE TWELVE WORST MISTAKES IN BUSINESS

THE TWELVE WORST MISTAKES IN BUSINESS

Herbert N. Casson

Tynron Press
England

This revised and updated edition published in 1995 by
Tynron Press
Unit 3 Turnpike Close
Lutterworth
Leicestershire LE17 4JA
U.K.

ISBN 1-85646-078-9

Cover design by Tony Chiang and Michael Wong
Typeset by Syarikat Cultural Supplies Sdn Bhd
Printed in Singapore by General Printing Services Pte Ltd

CONTENTS

Introduction

Preface

1. The Old Ways Are The Best 1
2. I Know My Own Business 11
3. I Have No Time To Read 20
4. Success Comes From Hard Work 23
5. I Take Things As They Come 29
6. Good Things Sell Themselves 35
7. I Cannot Afford To Pay High Wages 41
8. Machinery Is Too Expensive 48
9. Let Him Wait For His Money 53
10. The Public Expects Too Much 59
11. There's No Sentiment In Business 65
12. It Can't Be Done 70

INTRODUCTION

This book is not for theoreticians – those who merely teach or study business, but for practitioners – owners and managers of business companies, large or small, whose heads are not up in the clouds and whose feet are planted firmly on the ground. Casson imparts business acumen acquired through experience and proven on the shop floor and in the market place. He uses simple, forceful words, not the pseudo-technical jargon of most modern books on business.

Where necessary, statistics and examples have been revised and updated, but the points which Herbert Casson made and the practices which he advocated need no modification. They are timeless.

No one will be able to read this book without saying, many times, "Why, that's common sense! Why didn't I think of it before!" And that is the strength of all of Herbert Casson's books. Whatever your line of business, he teaches you how to increase net profits through measures directed by sound common sense.

PREFACE

Here is a collection of destructive old sayings that have almost certainly ruined more people in business than any other single thing. If you want to know why some 40,000 or so businesses in Britain have folded up in 1991, read the 12 chapters in this book.

In it you will find the main reasons why the large majority of people who go into business fail to make the grade. In it you will also find the 12 sayings that *are* deadly to the business community – sayings that can destroy character as well as profits.

There is a semblance of wisdom in these foolish sayings that are usually spoken in an oracular manner, as though they were unquestionable and cannot be challenged. Often, people believe in them sincerely in spite of their disastrous consequences.

As you will see, most of them are in the form of excuses. When people are doing badly, whether in business or anything else, they will come up with one of these sayings as a defence against criticism.

The real reason why they are doing badly may be that they are lazy or ignorant or unteachable or in the wrong line of business. But by coming up with one of these sayings as an excuse, they try to place the blame elsewhere for their misfortunes.

These 12 sayings or **mistakes** – which they are for the purpose of this book – have stood in the way of success and prosperity for lots of people long enough. The time has come to wipe them out of our minds and our conversations.

Once people have thoroughly cleared their minds of this rubbish – this make-believe wisdom – they will be ready to go forward and make a success of their lives.

Herbert N. Casson

CHAPTER 1

The Old Ways Are The Best

The belief in this saying has ruined millions of people. It is one of the oldest mistakes people make and one of the most universal as well. It appears to be indestructible and has the vitality of a superstition. It survives in spite of everything.

Today we have a world full of new things. Something we have never seen or heard of before surfaces before our eyes almost every day. We are dazzled by the success and the splendour of new discoveries, and yet tens of thousands of us sit in the midst of all this novelty and insist on saying: "The old ways are the best."

The reason for this is because people are usually fascinated by old things. Sentiment seems to grow proportionately to the age of things. The older the object or saying, the more sentiment is attached to it. The most irreplaceable building in London is Westminster Abbey, dedicated to the glorious dead. The British are apt to give the impression that they would sooner destroy an entire town than one of their ancient cathedrals.

This is a natural sentiment. It does no harm and creates patriotism. It ennobles us to remember and revere the heroes of the past and their monuments. But when this reverence for the past is bestowed upon antiquated machinery and business methods, it becomes destructive, absurd and absolutely unacceptable.

When every ancient thing is regarded as sacred, sanctity becomes a costly and dangerous obstacle in the way of progress. To look upon everything new as unwelcome is a sign of weak-mindedness. It is sheer folly. We tend to forget that age, like youth, has its follies too. And a dislike for new things is one of the common follies of the old.

It is clear that we should get our priorities right with regard to old things and old habits. I firmly believe that reverence for the old should be confined to things of sentiment and should not be bestowed upon anything connected with progress and the upliftment of the human condition.

For instance, a woman may want to preserve the going-away dress she wore on her wedding day, but it does not mean that she will want to wear the same style of dress all the time. Similarly, a man may become attached to a car that he bought 25 years ago, but it would be more economical and perhaps safer for him to keep it idle in his garage and buy a new car for daily use.

Britons invariably like to retain the old, but eventually get round to adopting the new. Their old institutions seldom end up on the scrap-heap. The entire British Isles is filled with survivals of the past. The London guilds still exist. The House of Lords goes on. Old creeds are not rewritten. The public schools still have their antiquated traditions. The Lord Mayor's Show has its annual parade through the streets of London. And so on.

No one objects to this. A nation must have its traditions. But traditions have no place in the office, the department store, factory, laboratory, supermarket or any other place of business.

The minds of young people in universities are constantly turned back to the past. When they eventually emerge into the world, many of them discover that they are hopelessly unprepared to grapple with the everchanging problems confronting it.

The past must be kept in its place. There should be no hand reaching out from the grave to stop the march of progress that goes on in the world of the living.

Nothing can be more futile and childish than to try to keep things as they were or as they are. Change rules the universe and we are all caught up in the whirl of it. It stimulates, creates and keeps things moving. Adherence to old things and methods does just the opposite – it mummifies. Life is a flux. It is a flame. It is a process. Nothing can ever compel it to remain the same.

Another thing to remember is this – no study of the past will equip us to pass judgement on what may or may not be done in the future. Those who live in the past are not qualified to talk about the new things that the present brings or the future may bring.

Things that were considered "impossible" a year ago are making their appearance in shops today. Every year brings new miracles in various fields, especially medicine and telecommunications. Still, there is always this chorus from the old fogeys – "It can't be done. The old ways are the best."

Nearly two centuries ago, these sceptics were ridiculing the attempts made to produce light without a wick. The answer, of course, was gas, and shortly thereafter the electric light made its debut. The same thing was asked about horse-drawn stagecoaches. "How can these coaches run by themselves?" they asked. The answer was the internal combustion engine.

How about ships sailing the seas without sails? Their predictable reaction? Impossible! Yet again, the steam engine made it possible. Later came ships driven by powerful turbines and today, by nuclear power.

Closer to our time, the old fogeys were firmly convinced that the propeller-driven aircraft had reached its limit in speed and height and could go no faster or higher. Of course they were proven wrong again when jet-propulsion, the discovery of new tough, light-weight, heat-resistant materials and other technological advances took aircraft to speeds and heights never dreamed of by man. And what about that "giant step" on the moon? "It simply cannot be done," they must have said, and were made to look fools not long after. Live coverage of world-wide events on television via satellites, and the remarkable advances made in computer and other sciences have made the world shrink even more in a relatively short space of time.

No doubt there are people today with the same "It can't be done" mentality, posing similar questions about developments in the future. It is always these sluggish people with memories instead of brains who will insist on playing the role of a doubting Thomas until someone comes along to prove them wrong.

These are the people with little or no imagination. They cannot accept change and will try their utmost to resist it as long as they can. They live mostly in the past and cannot foresee what the future can bring. They seem to be unconscious of this defect in themselves.

Such people are inclined to be old-fashioned. They do not fit into this high-speed century. They wear old-fashioned clothes and dislike any new time-saving device. Most of them abhor the computer. Some even detest escalators and are deadly afraid of flying in aircraft. They are sincere in all this and there is no reason why they should not be allowed to go their own simple way.

It is when such people sit on boards of big companies or inherit large fortunes that they are more than likely to be dangerous and destructive. Because they are hopelessly out of touch with the modern world, they more often than not "suffocate" and eventually destroy any company in which they have a major say.

They are not competent to run any organisation or sit on the board of any corporation. Neither are they qualified to deal with the public in these days of quick decisions and changes. To put it bluntly, the old ways and methods are the most dangerous and destructive. The most dangerous member of any board of directors is the person whose age compels respect, yet whose brain is primitive and undeveloped, and unable to comprehend effective new methods and influences in the business world today.

Is it not true that most of the new trades are prospering while many of the old ones are struggling to make small profits or break even? Are large profits not being made by the producers of hi-tech products like audio, video, computer and other electronic equipment? New companies that take risks have to contend with keen competition. They have to pay the high cost of pioneering. Most of them sell products considered as luxury items, not necessities. They have had to create a demand, and yet they are making big profits.

The main reason why new businesses are prospering is because they are quicker to adopt new ideas and methods. The old trades are handicapped by inert people running them and by old, worn-out methods of production and selling. They have fallen into a rut. The routine has slowed them down.

Age and experience ought to be an asset, not a drawback. A company that has been established for 50 years has an immense advantage over a company set up a year or two ago. If an old company keeps itself alert and alive, it can always do better than a new one. But if an old company allows its arteries to harden – if it becomes slow, old-fashioned and puffed up with its own dignity – then a much younger company with energy and drive can easily run circles around it.

A company is like a house. It must be continually renovated and practically rebuilt at least once in a generation. It must adapt itself to its changing environment or a liquidator will soon be at the door.

Once a company is known to be old-fashioned, its customers become wary of buying its goods. The key words in business today are **style** and **practicability**. Style means being up to date with the products, and practicability means selling products that people want and at prices that will make them irresistible.

How do you think a boutique would fare if it puts up an advertisement like this: "All the good old styles – take your pick of Victorian hats like those your great-grandmother wore!" It would be out of business in no time at all. At the other end of the scale are the manufacturers or retailers who pride themselves in selling up-to-the-minute goods, yet persist in using antiquated machinery and methods to make and sell them. This is a curious fact and difficult to explain.

Few people are consistent in their progressiveness. Their brains seem to have water-tight, or idea-tight compartments. One compartment may be progressive, while the other may be traditional or old-fashioned.

I have often asked manufacturers this question: "Why don't

you scrap this old machine and buy a new one?" Invariably, they reply with surprise: "Why? This machine has given us very good service for 25 years!" They apply the test of seniority to decide the value of a machine. It is difficult to convince them that a major or total breakdown of old machines could mean big losses in business.

My friend, a successful businessman, once told a story about a factory he bought. The previous owner showed him around the works, and when they arrived before a large piece of machinery, he said with great pride: "This machine was bought by my father 50 years ago. It was made for a ship, but for some reason wasn't put into one. My father bought it for a song, and it is still in good running order." However, the function of that machine remained a mystery. Nobody knew what it was used for. The first thing my friend did was to scrap that machine. Then he went on to reorganise the entire factory. He did not build up a large, successful organisation by using 50-year-old machines, and useless ones at that.

The fact is that people's reverence for age seems to overflow into the business compartments of their brains. When this happens, the result is disastrous. It makes them content, even proud, to carry on with old equipment and old methods. It cultivates a dislike in them for improvements and efficiency. It also prevents them from recognising talent among the young people in their organisations. It makes them obstructive and unteachable.

A manufacturer once said to me in a rather lordly and dictatorial way: "And do you think you can teach *me* anything?" I simply replied with another question: "What would you think of a member of your staff who put that same question to you?" He saw the point immediately and was quick to admit that he was unteachable. Like many leaders of large businesses, he had come to regard himself as the sole source of knowledge and authority.

Too many successful people in business become slovenly through complacency. This is the reason why so many of them seem to lose their grip as they get older. Their business acumen begins to fade. This in turn adversely affects their businesses and profits begin to shrink. They are beset by problem after problem. And all because they persist in holding fast to the "old ways" of doing business.

It is not easy to change the thinking of elderly people. It is natural for old people to prefer old ways. No magic potion can restore the vigour of youth to them. But they can be alerted to the fact that they are no longer as efficient and innovative as they once were. This will enable them to take steps to ensure that their companies do not go down the drain.

It will give them the opportunity to groom younger, talented and progressive people to take over the running of their organisations should the need arise. They will also have the opportunity to scout around for like-minded young and capable business people to be appointed as directors. They can learn to be less dictatorial, to delegate authority to younger people and to measure the value of members of their staff by enterprise, initiative and energy, as well as by age and experience.

In general, directors who are set in their ways and opposed to any change endanger their companies when:

1. they obstruct every suggestion for improvement;
2. they make no helpful suggestions;
3. they hold fast to methods that are out of date;

4. they do nothing to boost the profits of their companies and are content with small profits and even no profit at all;
5. competitors are forging ahead and they do nothing about it;
6. they do nothing to encourage their companies to adopt new ideas and methods to boost business.

Any director who is guilty of these six transgressions against his company, shareholders and workers should be classified as too old and useless in his job, whether he is 35 or 70.

I think it is generally accepted that there are old people with young ideas and young ones with old ideas. People of all ages have their abilities as well as defects; and any company that is run entirely by old or young people is more than likely to be run badly.

There is an eternal struggle between the old and the young, and the pity of it is that the old usually have the money and the authority. It would appear that the young are handicapped from the start.

The most able and wise of all people are those who have become old without losing the spirit of youth. When you see elderly people with capital who are still full of initiative and courage, you may be sure that any business they control will continue to grow and prosper.

When it comes to business methods and equipment, the test question is: "What purpose will it serve – is there any other way to get better results?"

No business method is sacred. We must assume that everything can be improved. There is nothing final in the methods of any well-managed company. Some manufacturers are so progressive that they can write off a third of the cost of their machinery every year. They do this, not to spend money unnecessarily, but to save it by reducing cost and speeding up output.

Nothing is more costly in any company than inertia. Those who "let well enough alone" have no idea how much this foolish policy is costing them. Old or outdated equipment that is not replaced inevitably means non-thinking employees – everyone jogging along in a rut. Output falls. Sales drop. Eventually, the company comes to a standstill. And this inevitably means bankruptcy.

Now and then, a nation as a whole wakes up and throws aside its "old ways". This proves that the "old ways" are not as firmly established as many might think. They can be abolished without disastrous consequences, and once they are discarded they are very seldom revived. The disastrous consequences that timid people predict do not happen. The "good old days!" No sensible person regrets them. They were probably days of hardship, poverty and clumsiness.

The human race is ripening, not rotting. The future will continue to bring thousands of improvements and luxuries such as we cannot imagine today. And the onus is on those in business to keep their minds open and receptive to new ideas as fast as they surface, and to adapt themselves and their companies to the torrent of change that is even now transforming the world.

CHAPTER 2

I Know My Own Business

There are relatively few people in business who can truly say: "I know my own business," and really mean it. Unfortunately, most people fondly believe or like to believe that they know everything there is to know about their business. They make one of the most common and most destructive mistakes in the business world.

"I know my business from A to Z," they say. But most of them are floundering with a superficial knowledge of what is going on in their organisations. The quality of a person's knowledge of a business depends on his teachability and the quality of his teachers. People who have good teachers and can adapt themselves easily will soon get to know a great deal about their businesses, but most of them pick up a smattering of knowledge and a good deal of misinformation from people who are not competent to teach anybody. Instead of boasting about their knowledge, they should forget it and proceed to learn from those who are successful in their trades.

There are no limits to human egoism. A few little commonplace ideas will give many people swelled heads. Four years at a university will often give a youngster an air of omniscience, and three or four years in a store, office or factory can often give an adult the belief that he has mastered his job and has nothing more to learn.

In spite of all the university courses in business administration and economics, the best test of a person's capability to do well in business is his or her ability to create goodwill and consistently produce good profits. The ability of such people should be judged by the results on their balance sheets and not by their paper qualifications.

Is it not true that business is the only game in which most of the players know little, but claim to know everything about the rules? The late British author Aldous Huxley once expressed this thought in a striking way.

He said: "Suppose it were perfectly certain that the life or fortune of everyone of us would, one day or other, depend upon winning or losing a game of chess! Don't you think that we should all consider it a primary duty to learn at least the names and moves of the pieces on the chessboard? Don't you think that we should look with a disapprobation amounting to scorn upon the father who allowed his son to grow up without knowing a pawn from a knight?"

Lots of people in business excuse their lack of training by saying: "My business is unique." The fact is that no business is unique. This is only an egotistical delusion. To say that a business is unique is only another way of saying that it is wholly independent of the rules and principles of the business world, which would be absurd. The truth of the matter is that anyone who claims to have a unique business is obviously ignorant of these rules and principles.

Three-quarters of any business is as common to one another as bees are to honey. Most of them can be standardised. They can be brought under control. They need not be run by whim, chance or personality.

What would we think of a singer who said: "My voice cannot be trained. It is unique." Or of a schoolboy who said: "I cannot be trained to run. My legs are unique." What would we think of a father who said: "My children must not be sent to school. They are unique."

The fact is that there are no goods in the world that cannot be advertised. There are no sales people who cannot be taught the principles of salesmanship. There are no factory workers who cannot be taught to be more productive. There is no genius who cannot be trained in something or other to a higher level of efficiency.

This idea of being unique is a conceited delusion. We all love to think that we are different and that the mould was broken when we were made. But the fact remains that the greater part of our brains and our bodies and our businesses is common and universal.

Very few business people see their business as a whole. The average person usually focuses his mind on one department. A person who is by nature a financier neglects the sales end of his business, just as a person who is by nature good at sales neglects the financial side.

A complete business brain requires not only an extensive knowledge of every aspect of a particular business, but also the ability to do every job in the organisation. There has never yet been, and will probably never be, anyone with a 100 per cent business brain.

This is one of the main reasons why many people fail in business. They fail to bring in people with the expertise they lack. They may be good as administrators, but if they don't have people who are good at marketing and sales, they will fail.

When a person dies, it is usually because one or more vital functions in the body has ceased to work. A person may be an athlete with a well-developed body and yet die of a weak heart. The same applies to a business – it is at the mercy of its weakest department or departments.

The job of a skilled manager or proprietor is not to know every detail of his business. He could not do this, without restricting the growth of his firm. His job is to engage people with various skills, lay down policy guidelines, and assess the results rather than dictate methods. He must engage people who are wiser than he is in their own lines. He buys knowledge and skill. He cannot pretend to have all the abilities that his business requires.

So you can see that it is a deadly mistake for a person to say oracularly: "I know my own business." He shuts the door on knowledge. He forgets that most of the knowledge required by any company must come from outside. Very little of it is homemade.

According to my "Formula of Progress", as outlined in another of my books called *Creative Thinkers*, "all progress depends upon the production of a comparatively small number of improved individuals, who are superior to the masses in knowledge, skill or character, and who, by reason of their superiority, render a new service to the mass of people among whom they live."

Even if a person is one of these "efficient few", his or her skill or knowledge is still limited. No one's brain is encyclopaedic. The wisest person must learn from other wise people.

Furthermore, it is a very strange fact of human nature that we are least likely to observe and study the things that are most common to us. What we see everyday, we do not really see. Very few people possess keen powers of observation, keen enough to really observe the ordinary things that happen in the course of a day's work.

Most people are almost automata with regard to their routine work. They go through eight hours a day in a trance. People can work for 30 years at a job and yet never once concentrate totally on what they are doing and how their work can be improved.

Merely working in a bank does not teach one everything there is to know about banking. Merely serving behind a counter does not teach a shop assistant how to sell goods efficiently.

Isn't it a fact that no one knows how to use his or her voice effectively without being trained by a voice specialist? Do we not have to be taught how to walk properly? Do we not have to go to a doctor when we are ill? Are most of us not almost wholly ignorant about our own bodies? Is it likely, then, that we can say that we know everything about our own businesses?

A young mother, with her first child, often resents the advice of older women. She says: "Don't I know how to care for my own baby?" The answer is – she does not. The high death-rate among babies in places where proper health care is lacking proves that. It is a very natural sort of egotism, but it is very dangerous.

Frank Gilbreth, a proponent of "motion study" early this century, proved that no bricklayers knew how to lay bricks efficiently. He found a way to speed up the process from 700 a day to more than 3,000. People had been laying bricks for centuries, but Gilbreth was the first person who studied the problem of laying bricks in the best way, and solved it.

Very few manufacturers know everything there is to know about every aspect of production in their factories. Their knowledge of their own business is usually amazingly superficial. When it comes to factory workers, their so-called "skill" generally consists of a few movements which they have learned, and which they perform day in and day out unthinkingly, as a trained seal beats a drum.

When American industrialist Henry Ford set out to make glass by a new continuous process, he was compelled to hire people who had no experience at all in glass-making. He discovered that the experience of glass-makers made them unsuitable for the new and better process.

Now that chemistry is so widely used in the manufacturing industry, almost every manufacturer would do well to re-learn his job. The chemist is creating new industries and revolutionising old ones.

Chemists have created a higher level of industrial knowledge. They can go into any factory and teach the works manager a better degree of accuracy and control of variables such as the works manager has never thought possible. They can teach farmers the most valuable facts about the soil and the crops.

Some people like to criticise others for seeking the services of outside experts, but their criticisms will eventually cost them dearly. One of the main reasons why large companies are able to cut costs and increase their sales is because they consider it worth their while to pay well for the advice of outside experts.

There are several good reasons why these experts can do much more to help a company than the people in it. They come with specialised knowledge gained from wide experience in advising many companies. They are independent and, consequently, do not have a narrow departmental outlook. Their job is to seek the welfare of the company as a whole and not just a particular section of it. And finally, they are not out to curry favour with anyone in the company in order to promote their self-interest.

Eventually, outside experts become successful in proportion to their independence and courage. They cannot afford to be afraid to tell their clients the truth – no matter how much it hurts at the time. In the long run, it is this sort of integrity that will establish and enhance the prestige of the experts.

The fees of experts are not that high in proportion to the results. Considered as a percentage of money saved, their fees are quite reasonable. A certain manufacturer I knew felt that he needed to extend his factory building considerably in order to boost production. The extension would cost him £1,800,000. But before he committed himself to the project, he decided to seek advice from an outside expert. The expert spent three weeks pouring over plans and speaking to members of the staff. Then he said to the manufacturer: "If you accept my plan to reorganise your factory to cut wastage and speed up production, you will not need to build the extension."

The manufacturer accepted his advice. The reorganisation cost him only £250,000. He saved £1,550,000 for not going ahead with his original plan. And output shot up dramatically. The expert's fee was only £4,000. I am sure he joined many others in their belief that there is nothing more profitable to an ailing company than the opinion of the right expert.

The vital principle of scientific management or rationalisation is that the job must be **studied**. That is why outside experts are so indispensable. They have studied the jobs, not merely worked at them. Frederick Taylor, who developed the principles of scientific management, once said: "Scientific management is not a theory to be applied to practice. It is a practice out of which a theory has developed."

Skilled experts have trained themselves to notice how work is being done. They study the various operations required for a job and time them. They are job builders. They have studied the cause of waste and how to reduce them. They know how to create new and better work-habits.

The difference between guesswork and research or motion-study work is amazing. Again and again, output has been doubled by outside experts. People who once said: "I know my own business," have been astonished to find that the output of their factories could be trebled using the same number of workers.

We are slowly beginning to appreciate **research**. This means coming up with facts and figures relating to a particular product or group of products, studying consumer habits in relation to them, and working out the best way to attract one to the other.

I have found that opinions are likely to be quite worthless in any business. Opinions are traditional. They are often the result of ignorance or laziness. No matter how many people believe in a thing, it may be untrue.

Many businesses are content to drift along in a haphazard sort of way. For the most part, this crazy patchwork of good, bad and indifferent work is created by the workers themselves. Usually, no one in a company is prepared to take the time or trouble to study it unless they are asked to do so, or an expert is brought in from outside to reorganise the entire system of work.

We have found in business life that self-reliance is a virtue up to a point. Beyond that point, there is no room for anything – not even knowledge – except sheer egotism and pride. Today, the wisest people consult the greatest number of experts. They learn from inside and outside their companies. In fact from everywhere – from other trades and professions, from science, from the arts, journalism and even from sports. They enrich their businesses with ideas and methods gathered from many countries. A new class of professional business people is being developed. The self-taught amateur does not have a ghost of a chance to compete against these new professionals.

The old-fashioned crude methods of manufacturing, selling and accountancy are today as much out of date as handcarts and sailing vessels. New techniques are constantly being developed and improved on – some long before the old ones have outlived their uses.

We are learning the vast possibilities of business skills. We are learning that it is more profitable to buy experience than to acquire it. There are so many things to learn these days that the span of one human life is too short in which to absorb all of it. Can one person learn everything about astronomy or mathematics or electricity in a lifetime? Can one person know everything about literature or music? In all the higher branches of learning, we must study what others before us have accomplished and try to make our own contributions to them. It is equally true of business today.

Someone once said: "So much to do, so little done." He might have added that a wise man would say: "So much to know, so little learned." So, isn't it time that we put an end to that preposterous and egotistical mistaken saying: "I know my own business."?

CHAPTER 3

I Have No Time To Read

As an experiment, I once asked four people to visit small shops in London to canvass for subscriptions to a magazine. As I expected, the response was poor. Of those who refused to subscribe, more than half gave this excuse: "I have no time to read." A significant answer, indeed. Much can be learned from "small", ordinary people as well as "big", successful ones.

The answer was one reason why they were small tradespeople – why they will always remain small and why they will go on struggling for a bare living. No time to read? No doubt, they were too busy wasting precious time everyday doing little profitless jobs, and fussing, worrying and labouring over trifling things. But they could not spare at least an hour a week to learn new and better methods of efficiency by reading books or magazine articles.

We expect to find a prejudice against "book-larnin" among the illiterate. We might expect that a dock worker, who makes a living by using his muscles and not his brains, would not appreciate the value of books and magazines. But these traders are business people. Their success depends upon their intelligence and yet they have "no time to read?"

A hundred years ago, there might have been some excuse for their aversion to reading. At that time there were hardly any business magazines around and very few practical books on business. Today, however, books and magazines on business abound in every bookshop. Books are today as indispensable to people in business as they are to professors or scientists. Ever since the mass production of printed matter nearly 200 years ago, reading has been the most powerful educational force in the world.

Hardly any famous people have reached where they are by saying: "I've got no time to read." The average person borrows or hires more books than he buys. But more and more people are beginning to appreciate the value of starting their own little libraries, no matter how small they may be.

More people are also learning to appreciate data – a vital word in every field of endeavour. There is now so much to know about business that ambitious people are compelled to read in order to know what other people in business are doing and what they are thinking about. It is very important for them to keep in touch with their particular trade or business field, and they cannot do this efficiently unless they do a lot of reading.

Take, for instance, chemists who come up with new materials or processes that could be of great significance to some industries, either as a means of improving product content or boosting production. It is obvious that people in these industries who take the trouble to read up on new discoveries and processes will be a couple of steps ahead of their competitors who have not kept abreast of things, simply because they have "no time to read". This short-sighted attitude could have serious consequences on their businesses.

People who don't take the trouble to read in these days of quick changes are as primitive as the cave dwellers of old. Such people sit in their little offices, with their imaginations, thoughts and ideas confined to the four walls of the building, knowing nothing of what is going on in the outside world, while their intelligent competitors beat them hands down in everything.

All the information people are looking for can be found in books today. Knowledge is no longer the preserve of a privileged few who had the means or the connections to gain access to it. The barriers that once surrounded knowledge are no longer there.

People who are practical and progressive never stop studying. They know that they cannot run their business using outdated methods. But there are still many business people in Britain and elsewhere who have a childish dislike for ideas and methods. What this dislike *costs* them in terms of money will probably never be known. Good ideas are like gold, and gold is where you find it. If the rest of the world learns from the English, why shouldn't the English learn from them too? In the export and import of ideas and methods, each nation should make sure that it gets as much as it gives.

Reading newspapers only is not enough. We must also read magazines and books. Every progressive and well-managed company today should have a reference library of sorts, no matter how humble it may be. Companies are well aware of the fact that their efficiency and profits depend, in the final analysis, upon the brain-power of their staff.

"No time to read!" What, then, is time for? How can any company hope to survive in these days of intense, world-wide competition unless it uses every possible means at its disposal to keep abreast of everything in this technological age of information?

CHAPTER 4

Success Comes From Hard Work

We frequently hear people say: "Success comes from hard work," and "If you want a thing well done, do it yourself!" Both are phrases of self-praise. Even business people pin medals on themselves. They are often as hungry for praise as people in show business. And if no one flatters them, they don't see anything wrong with doing it themselves.

The phrase "Success comes from hard work" is a dangerous half-truth. It is true that success comes from work, but not from work alone. What good is hard work alone without any kind of thinking, planning, managing and co-operation? To do these things well require ability, insight, a certain sensitivity and basic knowledge of psychology that goes way beyond that outdated "nose to the grindstone" attitude usually associated with the term "hard work".

There are many employers who were once employees and still have the brains and outlook of employees. They have no knowledge of the art of management and supervision. They are always physically busy.

Almost always their troubles increase. They get deeper and deeper into the mess. And just before they are completely overwhelmed, their energy is prodigious. They think they are business builders, but they are not. They are only bog-builders. Nothing that they do is well done.

These people invariably sneer at anything that has to do with efficiency – lectures, books and staff training. They are too busy with meaningless things. It is not too difficult to spot the type – they can be found everywhere.

There is one simple fact that disproves the saying – "Success comes from hard work." It is that the mass of people work hard and most of them are not well-off. The mass of people are not physically lazy. They are industrious. Yet they are not rich.

Surely no one wants the toiling masses to toil harder. To toil means the sheer use of muscle – the body at work and the mind idle. Horses toil, but human beings should not. Have not inventors and scientists been wracking their brains in the last century and a half to take the burden of toil off the backs of human beings and put it on engines and machines?

It is a strange fact that if you leave a worker to himself, he will almost always work in the hardest way. Workers have usually been opposed to machinery and all labour-saving devices and methods since the advent of the industrial age. And there are still many who labour under the delusion that machinery will deprive them of their jobs.

In lots of factories and other places of work, you will invariably see people using their weaker instead of their stronger muscles to work. You will see them in all sorts of strained and most uncomfortable positions. They lift and carry weights that could seriously affect their health. They really "put their backs into it." It would be better if they put their heads into it instead. As my shrewd old grandmother, who did not have much of an education, used to say: "Use your head to save your heels."

Efficiency means a higher percentage of result. It means doing more with less effort. It does not mean more sweat. It means finding out the best, the quickest, the easiest and the cheapest way to do something.

A story is told of a wealthy New Yorker who bought a newspaper. He went into the office one afternoon and found all the reporters out. "If they don't stay at their desks, I'll sack the lot," he fumed. "I don't think you should do that," advised the managing editor. "This is a morning paper. I would certainly recommend that they be sacked if I found them in the office now. They are not here at this moment simply because they are doing their jobs – out covering the news."

Little by little, the efficiency experts are taking the fuss and drudgery out of industry. They are introducing new methods and systems that do jobs very well, very quickly, very easily and very economically.

Decades ago, efficiency expert Frederick Taylor was the first person to come up with "rationalised" production – a way of reducing the number of motions required to complete one or several operations to the barest minimum without sacrificing quality and using less energy. Known also as time-motion studies, it is a common tool today for people in business, especially manufacturers finding ways to boost output.

Similarly, Gilbreth studied the whole process of bricklaying, and finally reduced the motions from 18 to 5. He enabled a bricklayer to do more than four times as much work using less energy.

This is how scientific management works. No slogging. No sweating. No drudgery. This concept of work reduces energy spent to a minimum, leaving the heavy work to be done by machinery and power.

Another management technique that employers have found effective in increasing productivity is the offer of incentives to employees whose work is outstanding. Some bosses treat their employees more like partners than salaried workers. They go out of their way to develop their abilities and ensure their loyalty. Progressive employers today believe in management-sharing. They no longer bother with every little detail, shun routine work, and concentrate on planning, policy and emergencies. They delegate authority among members of their staff who are competent to do the job.

One merchant I know has delegated his responsibilities so efficiently among the senior members of his staff that his company now practically runs itself with hardly any interference from him. He devotes only three to four months of the year to it and spends the rest of his time abroad looking for new contacts and ideas.

He began with a small shop and now has a business worth at least £60,000,000. He does not believe that success is necessarily the product of only hard work. Rather, he attributes success mainly to "perfecting one's organisation and gathering new knowledge."

The modern employer is a staff-trainer who does not keep his knowledge to himself like some sort of trade secret. He does not try to monopolise anything and helps in the development of the younger, up-and-coming members of his staff. He is appreciative, not jealous. And he does all he can to increase the brain-power of his managers and employees.

Something people in business should always remember is that no company can be more efficient than the total amount of efficiency put into it by its employees. As far as possible, it should be the aim of employers to make every employee feel special – to give everyone a sense of being responsible for a portion of the company's work and success.

A smart director once told me: "The measure of a manager's value is his ability to put people in charge of various departments who are more capable in their line of work than he or she is."

In short, the main purpose of business leaders is to build up their organisations, not to get involved in petty manners or the daily routine, except when it comes to formulating important policy decisions. Their job is to issue directives, not carry them out. This may seem simple and self-evident, but a lot of employers find this difficult to do. That is why their companies cease to grow.

Some of the most successful people in business today make it a practice to manage their organisations from a distance. They shy away from the monotonous daily details. To get a better perspective of things, they prefer to take a bird's-eye view of their organisations – concentrating only on important policy matters and future developments. They use their brains, something all fussy, small-minded people shirk.

The harder a person's job is, the more he or she should take time to think, instead of creating a turmoil of activity. People cannot think clearly when they are working frantically at a job. They cannot see the wood for the trees when they are swamped with petty details.

Life, I find, is too serious to take it seriously. It masters you if you cannot face it with a smile. There must be some room for relaxation in the midst of all that concentration. At times, when I have been overwhelmed with problems and responsibilities, I have found it relaxing and soothing to break away from my cluttered desk and go out to see a show, take a brisk walk or relax in a restaurant. Eventually, I turn the bothersome problems over in my mind and very frequently either find the solutions or realise that they are not worth bothering about.

Invariably, I find that when people make decisions while they are burdened with worry, fear or overwork, their decisions are likely to be bad ones. No one's brain can function properly when it is clogged up with worry, anger or fear. Neither can people take a larger view of a business problem when they are too preoccupied with the details of it.

A new type of people in business has emerged. They are very different from the Mr. Know-it-all-and-do-it-all type of days gone by. They know that the function of those at the top of a business organisation is to teach, to lead and to organise.

Development! Growth! These are big words – bigger in meaning and content than the word "work". Thousands of people in business fail because they have little or no time to devote to development or growth. How can people make their companies grow or develop when they are already too "big" for them because they permit small, petty matters to occupy their minds to the exclusion of everything else?

The stormy seas of business today are too rough for the little boats. The tiny shop with two assistants and the factory with 20 workers have little chance of surviving in competition with large factories and organisations. A healthy business must grow, and it can only do so if the owner studies the laws of growth and organisation. Drudgery leads only to more drudgery. It can never lead to success.

CHAPTER 5

I Take Things As They Come

This is what a happy-go-lucky person would say – just the opposite of the one described in the last chapter. This saying may sound alright to a shallow mind. The person who says it expects admiration. It makes someone who says it appear to be big and invulnerable, like the Rock of Gibraltar. "No matter what comes, I shall be able to take care of myself" – that is what the person who says it implies.

To take things as they come? No doubt about it – they will come. And when they do, they will bowl over those who smugly and complacently believe that nothing can shake them or pull them down. And a very appropriate epitaph for their dead business would be – "Here lies Smith or Jack or Tom. He took things as they came."

It is a fact that there are some easy-going people who prefer a carefrce life to wealth. They prefer a small, struggling business to a large, prosperous one. They dislike a strenuous, stress-filled life. They will avoid all responsibilities if they can get away with it. They have no ambition whatsoever.

These people may be wise. They may have hobbies which they value more than wealth. But what I want to point out is that they should not be in business at all. Smoking a pipe is fine, but a man cannot smoke a pipe while he is playing football. Such people should be dentists, barbers, civil service clerks or postmasters. They should not be in the hurly-burly of business life, which is always risky and strenuous.

An easy-going disposition makes for happiness, but not for financial success. A take-things-as-they-come person is likely to be a kind husband or father, but his wife and children will do well to learn how to support themselves. He will be beloved by his neighbours and friends, but not by his creditors.

This easy-going spirit in business is universal. It is common in the East as well as the West. "What will be, will be," say the fatalists or, "We will cross those bridges when we come to them," say many people in business. These sayings have ruined thousands. They are not wise nor true and never were. It is always better to study than to guess. It is always wise to look forward and prepare for possible dangers. Stoicism has its value, but it is a virtue only up to a point. The main thing in life is not endurance. It is the mastery of circumstances. We reach the highest point of power when we decide what shall happen, not when we merely endure the blows that fall upon us.

Indifference does not mean intelligence. It means a blend of laziness and lack of imagination. It is a defect. It cannot rightly be called courage or hardiness. It is a kind of inertia. After all, people are not stones. They are conscious and perishable.

The Spanish have a fatal word, "Manana", meaning tomorrow. It has given them the habit of procrastination that took them out of the first league of nations. The Russians have the word, "Nichevo", meaning "what does it matter?" and look where it got them today. The British, too, have a phrase "Wait and see", which compels them to pay an enormous price for being unprepared.

There is also that much-misused word – "Hope", that has given people an excuse for delay and idleness. Hope is a passive word. Usually it means resignation, and resignation means surrender. It is only when people have done all that they can to overcome their difficulties that they have a right to use that word.

Too many people in business are drifting into an unknown future. They have no plan, no policy, no definite purpose. There are hundreds of such people who do not know what their day's work will be until they read their correspondence. They are pushed through the day by letters and telegrams.

They are inert. They move only by outside pressure. They fritter away their time on jobs that could be done by clerks. At the end of the day, no real executive work has been done. Their day has been cut up into little bits and not one hour of it has been used for important work.

Someone once said that "Our English motto is **be thorough**." I wish it were. Too many of us do not know what thorough means. We think that it means persistence and endurance. But that is only half of it. It means getting ready before we begin to work. It means looking ahead and preparing for difficulties before they arise.

Once we have begun a task, we are unconquerable and patient. We are the wonder of the world at keeping our noses to the grindstone. We "stick it out" to the last drop of blood. But have we been noted for our research – our foresight – our ability to make plans in advance?

It is the very essence of managerial work to look ahead and make plans for the coming year. Ordinary workers do not need to do this. They think only of the day's job. A foreman thinks of the week's tasks. A works manager thinks in terms of months and a managing director must look as far ahead as he can. His success depends largely on his ability to project the future in terms of years and to prepare for them.

Science, as we know, means precision. It turns us all into fortune-tellers. We are able to predict what will happen when two chemicals are mixed together. We are even able to predict an eclipse to the minute.

We can predict the weather accurately, pin-point and track the movements of storms, hurricanes and typhoons. And because of them, thousands of lives on land and at sea are saved. We have forecasts of crops and know well in advance, barring any unforeseen disaster, what the harvest will be like.

We also have forecasts of the price movements on the stock exchanges in the main trading centres of the world. We have charts that show previous rise and fall of prices and we know that there are wave movements in prices that precipitate booms and depressions.

There is no information more valuable than the knowledge that certain rises and falls in prices will probably take place. If I had one wish granted to me by a kindly genie, I would ask to know the price movements on the stock exchange just one hour in advance. Then, with the aid of half a dozen brokers, I could proceed to buy and sell myself into a fortune.

Step by step, science has moved into the business world. It has helped us to predict future business trends more or less accurately. We are no longer making blind guesses.

It is common practice now for companies to try to project their sales figures a year or more in advance. Most companies prefer planning towards steady growth rather than take unnecessary risks that could break them. What companies fear most is sales that fluctuate wildly for no apparent reason – up one minute and down the next, making nonsense of the "on" and "off" sales seasons.

For this reason every well-managed company today has a department that deals with the planning of every aspect of sales promotion, including market research. Everything about a company's performance is scientifically studied before decisions are taken on how to proceed with any plan or project.

For instance, one of the tests of an efficient factory is keeping strictly to its delivery dates. A factory cannot pass this test without the help of a planning department. The most perfect development of planning is, perhaps, the operation of a railway or underground subway. The running of every train is planned in advance. Schedules are worked out down to a minute, or even seconds. Time-tables are drawn up and if you are a little late for a particular train you want to catch, you will very likely miss it. There is no guesswork. Every movement is planned in advance. Nothing is left to chance.

Then there is personal planning. The most practical way of keeping track with appointments, addresses, birthdays, telephone numbers and a host of other things is either to keep a diary or store it in one of the little marvels of the electronic world – an organiser. Busy people who are constantly on the move prefer to use the electronic organiser. A cross between an electronic calculator and a laptop computer, it will store in its "memory" everything you key into it. Slim and a little bigger than the hand, it will even keep track of your business projects.

Most progressive companies nowadays keep a list of events, appointments, projects, etc. well ahead of time. They store such information in the memory banks of their office computers. Business people who travel extensively, however, will also transfer such information into a laptop computer, which is no bigger than a small attache case and much more versatile than an electronic organiser.

The objective of all this, of course, is to prevent matters from being overlooked, forgotten or done in a last-minute scramble. Above all, the important point to remember is that the more people plan ahead, the more they are able to control things.

We do not need to drift along as helplessly as a lot of us used to do in days gone by. By taking thought and planning, we can add many cubits to the stature of our businesses. Take fashion, for instance. It can be foreseen to a certain extent. There are tendencies in style that can be observed. Fashion is created, not born. It is created from many influences in various countries. Those who study it and know the sources from which it comes, can now and then guide it and decide what it will be in the coming year. Fashion is always more or less of a gamble, but the risks can be greatly reduced by study and foresight.

It is clear that although companies cannot accurately foretell future trends, they no longer need to run their businesses aimlessly. Scientific management now allows them to catch glimpses of what they can reasonably expect around the next corner.

Gradually we are learning to exert a greater measure of control over things that affect our daily lives in a way our forefathers never dreamed of. The old-fashioned casual way of doing business has now become dangerous.

CHAPTER 6

Good Things Sell Themselves

There is a very common belief that those who rose to the top reach there on merit alone. Having known many people who made it to the top, and many who never got off the bottom rung of the ladder of success, I am compelled, in the interest of truth, to say that this is not true. However, I wish it were.

I have seen the wicked and dishonest flourish shamelessly and the righteous and deserving forgotten and ignored. I have seen foolish people elected to the highest office and I have seen the most able people die in obscurity.

No one who has used his or her eyes can say that public opinion is just, or that merit is eventually rewarded. Is it not true that the newspapers with very large circulations are often the trashiest, and that the so-called "best-selling" books are usually the silliest of the year? And through the ages, have not many of the most able and noble of men and women been allowed to languish in obscurity and starve? Have there not been nations that set upon their wisest and most useful people, as though they were criminals? Have we not had, over and over again, persecutions of the wise and virtuous?

All over the world there are highly capable people doing menial and insignificant jobs. Why? Because they do not know how to sell themselves. They have the mistaken belief that merit sells itself – that if they sit back long enough it will eventually be recognised. This seldom, if ever, happens. Nobody gets the wealth and fame they deserve unless they know how to market their abilities or their goods.

I think we have all heard of the man who stood on London Bridge and offered golden sovereigns at sixpence each. He sold only one. And the person who bought it did not believe it was gold. He bought it as a gift for his little girl. Didn't Schubert sell his immortal compositions for a shilling apiece? Didn't Dr. Samuel Johnson receive only enough to keep body and soul together while he worked on his dictionary of the English language? Haven't many inventors received nothing at all for their inventions?

If this is true with people, is it not equally true with products? If ability will not sell itself, is it likely that high quality goods will sell themselves? Do we not, in both cases, need to rely on **salesmanship** to sell them?

Salesmanship is the art of attracting favourable attention to merit or goods. It is the art of creating appreciation in the minds of the public – of making people notice things, desire them and want them.

By means of salesmanship, we call attention to the quality points of our products. We maintain our prices by showing value. We make this value conspicuous in all manner of ways. We adapt our products to many markets. Either we study what people want, or we teach them to want what we make.

And to supplement salesmanship, a new method of selling called **advertising** made its debut in the business world. We might say that it is a sort of mass production salesmanship. It appeals to the public as a whole, or to certain large sections of the public, instead of to the individual or small group of individuals via a sales person. There are very few people, perhaps none, who can recall the early days of advertising. American merchant John Wanamaker was the first businessman to take out full-page advertisements in newspapers. He died in 1922. Mr. Wanamaker was certainly a wise man who knew more clearly than anyone in his day that good things do not sell themselves.

In its early days there were some unscrupulous people who misused advertising. A lot of it was misleading and fictitious. It had a bad start, so much so that it was some time before reliable companies were prepared to use it. Little by little, however, it came into the hands of more responsible people who use it to educate, not cheat, the public. Today, it is safe to say that more than anything else, it is advertising that provides the bulk of revenue for magazines and newspapers.

It can now be seen that we need not sit down and wait for the slow approbation of the public. Life is too short for that. We can now make a company, store or shop well-known in a couple of weeks, even days; we can take an unknown product or article and make it famous in a very short time – and all through advertising.

Newspapers give us the news of the day. Advertisements give us the news and opinions concerning the goods and services that are being offered for sale. We know the power of news. We know that it can make or break governments. We know that it moulds public opinion, the power behind all thrones. And now we know the power of advertising when it comes to selling things.

Advertising makes goods famous, and people love to buy famous things. They like to book seats at the opera, cinema or concerts, or check into rooms at first class hotels, travel on luxury liners or enjoy themselves at the most expensive holiday resorts. They pay incredible prices for paintings by the Old Masters and price is no object when they set their hearts on buying designer articles or apparel.

Advertising makes goods popular. It brings them into the conversation of the day. It coins new words and enables manufacturers to have a monopoly of their own brands.

The dominant fact about selling goods is this – a demand for them has to be created. This demand does not spring up of itself. The public will not automatically rush to buy any new product that appears on the market. On the contrary, they are inclined to be suspicious about anything new that has yet to be tried and proven to be good. They have to be taught and convinced through advertising that a particular product is just what they need.

When the telephone was invented by Alexander Graham Bell, was it welcomed? It was not. It was called a "scientific toy". Bell, a Scotsman, took it to England and could find no one to invest money in it. It was offered to the Americans for 16 months before it caught on. It was the same for the invention of the air-brake and the sewing-machine. People wanted nothing to do with them at first. So the inventor had to literally go out and "sell" them to the sceptics – and doing that often required as much ability and energy as it did to invent them. Remember, there was no such thing as advertising in those days.

Take insurance policies. Few will quarrel with the necessity to protect families from want when their breadwinners die. Or the wisdom of providing for medical expenses in old age in these days of rising medical costs.

Yet, do we see people rushing to insurance offices to take out policies for such emergencies? Are there queues outside insurance companies waiting to buy policies? No. Is it not true that insurance companies train their agents to put across the shrewdest and most persistent sales pitch in order to sell their policies?

It is certainly not an easy task these days to be a good sales manager or be involved in any capacity connected with selling. With a multitude of products flooding markets, with such keen competition in price and quality among producers of the same products, it is difficult to find new markets, let alone create a demand for them. This is the problem that haunts all people connected with sales. It is also worth noting that all industrialised nations are capable of producing more than they can sell. And more often than not they do.

Sales managers have the difficult task of creating new national habits and of dealing with one of the inevitable consequences of competition – price-cutting. They must not only sell. They must sell at a profit. A sales manager must, to a certain extent, be a showman. He must know how to attract the favourable attention of the public. Quite often, he may need to use "gimmicks" to boost sales. He may have to do something spectacular or give away free samples to the public.

In some way, sales managers must dramatise their goods and attract customers, the more influential and well-known the better. They cannot afford to sit in their offices and wait for orders to come to them. In short, they must use every means available at their disposal to woo people to look at and buy their products.

The public is generally hostile to most things that are radically new and different. Even if it is not hostile, it is indifferent. People are usually settled in their buying habits. Therefore, skill is required to put across a new line of products on the market.

Striving for originality in advertising is the key to successful sales campaigns. The same thing applies to all other methods of selling. You either keep up with the competition or surpass it, or you will end up by the wayside. Selling costs keep soaring, but the fact still remains that nothing costs as much as oblivion. How to escape from oblivion – how to keep selling costs to a minimum and win over the buying public – still remains one of our most difficult problems.

CHAPTER 7

I Cannot Afford To Pay High Wages

We often hear employers say: "I cannot afford to pay high wages." How do they know they can't? They have never tried to do so. They have always paid low wages. They do not know that underpaying workers is likely to be most unprofitable and seldom worth it. Or that the most costly workers are likely to be the most profitable. They do not know the difference between ability and ignorance.

To many employers, the most important thing in business is to keep the cost of wages down to the barest minimum. They regard payment of wages as a decrease of profits. The directors of a London firm once actually terminated the services of its highly-paid managers – from the managing director down. The urgent need to economise was given as the reason behind the move. Later, they admitted that it was a suicidal thing to do.

Too many employers classify wages in the same class with taxation. They would like to lower both wages and taxes. This is a mistake, and many companies have been wrecked by it. Paying taxes is, of course, not the same thing as paying wages.

I knew one employer who did not mind hiring a few extra workers so long as he paid them what he thought was a fair wage – a flat rate of £50 a week. He would have had a fit if anyone asked him for twice that amount, but that was exactly what his competitors were paying their workers for faster and better results – with prospects for advancement. Naturally, this employer had to be content with a high turnover of the better ones were leaving him to join his sequently, performance at his plant began to ›ut fell drastically and he found himself in difficulties.

Money spent on wages, machinery, office equipment, business books, staff training, advertising, etc., is like seed sown in good soil. It all comes back in the form of bigger profits and better dividends. It is productive. It's all worthwhile.

A neglected, untrained, discontented, poorly-paid employee is not profitable. He does very little work, and what little he does is done badly. A newly-hired worker is not necessarily productive, but potentially so. It is the job of his company to make him productive by providing good training, good pay and good equipment.

Some years ago, a company had union trouble and decided to hire foreign workers with little or no experience. Without any training, they were put to work. The whole factory was soon in trouble. Machines constantly broke down. Output dropped and profits were wiped out. Eventually, the company was forced to liquidate. If ever an organisation deserved what it got, this was it.

How can it be a wise policy to put costly machinery into the hands of cheap, unskilled workers? How can profits be made when poorly-paid shop assistants, who know next to nothing about sales, are allowed to deal with customers?

Every store, supermarket or shop has its list of "dead" customers. Why are they called "dead"? Because of the errors, discourtesy or the stupidity of poorly-paid so-called sales people. Unquestionably, these are the main reasons for the high "death-rate" among customers in many of these establishments.

Employers should chalk up the number of "dead" customers in the form of "error losses" so that they will know how much their employees are costing them in lost sales. Breakages through carelessness is another area that can be quite costly to hotels and restaurants.

Then there is the cost of supervision. This has to be added to wages. The most competent workers need little or no supervision. They are reliable and skilled. As to the question of limit for salaries and wages, the answer is that there is no limit. There is no limit to ability and usefulness. Everything, of course, depends on the type of job, the level of skill required, the responsibility it carries, etc.

There are efficient and inefficient people. They should be graded not by how much money they have or what position they hold because both can be obtained accidentally. Grading should be based on character, intelligence, efficiency, honesty and value to the community. I do not believe in class distinction, but in leadership and the grading of human talent. I believe in the survival of the fittest.

"That salesman is worth his weight in gold to me," said a manufacturer, pointing to an energetic young man. He added: "That statement is literally true. He is one of my best salesman. He weighs 68 kilogrammes, and in terms of gold, that would be worth about £150,000. The interest on that amount at 6 percent is £9,000 a year, which is less than what I pay the salesman."

At a certain company, an office safe was out of order. It could not be opened. An expert was called in, and he opened it in ten minutes. "How much do I owe you?" asked the owner of the safe. "One hundred pounds," replied the expert. "That is too much. I refuse to pay it," said the safe-owner. The expert closed the door of the safe, locked it and said, "Very well, you can open the door yourself."

He was about to leave the office when the safe-owner called him back and said: "Alright, I want you to open the safe door." Said the expert: "That will cost you £150 now. I do not charge for time spent but for expertise." And so the owner of the safe agreed and had to pay an additional £50 for not appreciating expert service.

One of the top salesman of a London company returned from a business trip to Paris and presented his bill for £1,500 – for expenses incurred during the trip – to the cashier. "This is ridiculous," said the cashier. "I cannot pay this amount until the boss approves it." So the salesman saw the boss who agreed with the cashier. He said: "You must be crazy to present such a bill for only a two-day stay in Paris." In a rage, the salesman snapped: "You can keep your job," and walked out of the office.

The boss decided to find out how much the company benefited from the two-day trip to Paris in terms of orders, and was struck dumb when he discovered it was worth £270,000. Straightaway, he instructed the cashier to call up the salesman and give him what he asked plus another £1,500 as bonus, in addition to his usual commission.

Three brothers left their farm to work in the city, and all managed to get jobs in the same company starting out with the same salary doing essentially the same work. Six years later, one was getting £500 a month, another £750 and the third £1,500.

Their father decided to visit his sons' employer to find out why there was such a disparity in their salaries for doing the same type of job. "I will call them in one by one and let them give you the reason for the difference in their salaries," said the employer.

So he called in Jim, the lowest-paid of the three, and said: "I understand the vessel Oceanic has just docked. Please go down and get an inventory of her cargo." Four minutes later, he was back in the office. He said: "She carries a cargo of 8,000 seal-skins. I got the information from the first mate over the telephone." "Thank you, Jim," said the employer. "That will be all."

He called in Frank, the £750 man, and said: "Frank, I want you to go down to the docks and get an inventory of the Oceanic's cargo." An hour later, Frank was back with a list showing that the Oceanic not only carried seal-skins, but also 500 beaver and 1,000 mink pelts.

The employer then summoned George, the highest-paid son, and gave him the same instructions. George still had not returned when the office closed for the day three hours later, but his father and employer waited for him. Finally he showed up half an hour later and said: "The Oceanic carries 8,000 seal-skins. They are selling at £20 each, so I took a two-day option on them, and I wired a prospective buyer in St. Louis, offering them to him at £30 each. I expect to receive his order tomorrow. There were 500 beaver pelts which I sold over the telephone at a profit of £2,600. The mink pelts are of poor quality, so I decided to have nothing to do with them."

"Very good," said the employer. When he left, the employer turned to the father and smiled. "You probably noticed," he said, "that Jim did not do as he was told; Frank did, while George did more than what he was told to do."

Studies have shown that some sales people can be six or seven times more effective than their less dedicated colleagues.

An association of 21 car dealers made a study of their sales people and came up with some interesting results. They found that, of those selling high-priced cars, 59 percent made 83 percent of the sales. Of these top sales people, all had been with their companies for at least two years.

Of those selling medium-and low-priced cars, 24 percent made 56 percent of the sales, and again all with at least two years' experience. The two best sales people sold as many cars as the 18 who sold the least. This is an indication that for every nine mediocre or inferior sales people, one exceptional one will emerge. It was found that those working on straight commission sold the most cars, while those on a fixed salary sold the fewest.

Some people are worth £60,000 a year. Some half that amount. There are quite a few in the United States whose yearly income, plus bonus, etc., are in the upper reaches of six figures and a few pull in seven, or even eight figures. Those in this rarefied stratum are the chairmen and chief executive officers of large corporations. In the long run, poorly-paid employees adversely affect the performance of their companies – they lower quality, destroy goodwill, increase costs and reduce profits.

The main reason for low output, listless workers, low wages and small profits is that a good proportion of wage workers are simply putting in time and not trying to really find out how much work each one of them can do. Most of them have not been tested nor graded by the quality and quantity of their work, as they should be.

If they stay at the job and don't drop dead before closing time, they can collect a day's pay. Very few are interested in asking themselves, "How much have I done?" It is like a game of football without a referee. It creates slackers, time-killers and dull-eyed drudges.

How can people be interested in what they are doing if nobody pays any attention to how much they do? Or to how well they do it? How can there be any skill or speed in a factory when skill and speed do not make any difference in the pay packet?

It has been discovered through experiments that people on piece-work do twice as much or more than those working on a time basis. People paid by the week are usually running at half-speed. By our stupid system of payment, we have trained workers to believe that every job must be made to last as long as possible. The cost of wages added on the products have almost priced them out of the market.

The fact is that all wages should, in some way, be based on results – either on work done or on net profits. Every worker should work on some sort of commission system. A person should be paid £200 a week if he earns it, and another only £50 a week if he is worth only that.

A wise policy for every employer is to make wages a fair percentage of earnings to provide every possible labour-saving device to enable his employees to earn more. Help them to make more money. An extra £20 a week means more than anything else to the average worker. Nothing pays off as well as having a staff of loyal, contented, diligent employees, free of money troubles and giving their all to their jobs.

CHAPTER 8

Machinery Is Too Expensive

Some people, particularly artists and those opposed to any form of change, are inclined to turn up their noses at the use of machinery to do anything. Perhaps they are repelled by the cold, impersonal way they function. Of course, from the aesthetic point of view, there is not much to be said in their favour.

But I have never been able to understand why machinery ought to be beautiful or, at least, pleasing to the eye. We might as well expect them to be fragrant. Surely, anyone who looks at a machine and tries to visualise a rose or a sunset must be a very foolish person.

Some idealists think that machinery dulls and brutalises the minds of workers. They denounce the "monotony" of repetitive work. They dislike the noise of machinery and the necessary imposition of discipline on the factory floor. But they forget the brutality and cruelty which have always existed in countries that use little or no machinery. They forget the slavery and child labour which industrialisation helped to abolish.

All this is to be expected. But what is surprising is that there are some so-called business people, especially in Third World countries, who look upon machinery as a necessary evil. They sit in the offices of their unprofitable little factories and say to themselves: "Machinery is too expensive. Why waste money installing them when I can hire cheap labour to turn out my goods by hand?" or "Why waste money replacing my machines with newer, faster and more efficient ones? The ones I have now are in working order and can last me at least another ten years."

These people can't see further than the tip of their noses. In a competitive world of mass production, some of them still cling to their craftsman-like attitude, preferring to produce their goods laboriously instead of swiftly and efficiently by machines.

These "manufacturers" mistakenly believe that their small, poorly-equipped, struggling, debt-free businesses are safe. They cannot understand how dangerous it is to conduct business this way, and that slowly but surely they will either be pushed out of the competition or swallowed by larger, more efficient organisations.

These "factories" are not, in a strict sense, factories at all. They are merely small workshops, and there is a big difference between the two.

A factory turns out products in bulk by division of labour and repetitive work through the use of machines. On the other hand, a workshop makes goods in small quantities mostly by hand, with very little machinery or division of labour. A workshop can and does make a single article. A factory never.

The ideal factory is like a watch. It is full of specialised machinery and workers. When 300 workers co-operate to make 250,000 pairs of shoes yearly by machinery – that is a factory. When one shoemaker makes one pair of shoes by hand in three days – that is a workshop.

A well-built factory is a complete process under one roof. It usually manufactures one product – possibly in a number of sizes – over and over again, with the least possible amount of hand-labour.

A manufacturer today is a capitalist. A factory is not a workshop. It is a place of big output, and big output requires the latest machinery. There are would-be manufacturers who are afraid to borrow enough money to buy up-to-date machinery to replace their out-of-date, rickety ones. They have a morbid fear of debt. They do not realise that money is the cheapest thing in the world. It probably does not occur to them that labour could cost four times as much as machinery.

It is manpower and not machine time that costs most. Wages and salaries are the big items in costs. A job that takes ten hours to do by hand can be done in a matter of minutes by a machine.

It is machinery that reduces manufacturing costs and increases output. Articles formerly sold at £10 each can now be had for £1, because of the cheapening influence of machinery. A stroll through your neighbourhood store will convince you of this truth.

Manufactured goods can no longer be made likc Persian rugs. This is an age of standardisation. Goods are now made for the masses, rather than for a wealthy few. Prosperity has been democratised to such an extent that even luxury items, once only the preserve of the rich, are now being bought by the ordinary man in the street.

When a manufacturer makes a few million articles, all exactly alike, he can afford to put his machines in line and clear the deck for action. He can afford to study every operation and every type of material used. He must strive to save seconds in time. If he saves a second on one operation, he has probably saved 34 eight-hour days. If each article costs £1 to produce and he saves one pence in the material cost per article, he has saved around £10,000 for every one million articles produced. Such is the cost-cutting power of mass production.

Also, when one million articles, all alike, are being produced, a manufacturer can implement a system of mechanical handling – chutes, conveyors, trucks, cartons, etc. – which will eliminate physical handling. He can make the materials and parts flow through the factory like a river. He can afford to use nothing but specialised tools and machines. Mass production is the only efficient way to manufacture goods that are meant for sale to the general public.

Even most of our office work now can be done by machines. Gone are the days when clerical and routine work, and even more sophisticated jobs, were done by people sitting on high desks – not unlike that found in schools – writing in big bound books or ledgers with old-fashioned pens.

An efficient office now has dozens of cost-saving machines. There are electronic typewriters, word-processors, powerful computers, printers, copiers, fax machines, shredders and all sorts of other high-tech machinery and communication systems. Air-conditioning helps to enhance the working environment, and to boost efficiency and productivity by maintaining the right temperature and humidity in offices, factories and laboratories.

All these working "aids" of human ingenuity cut costs in the long run. They save. People who look upon them as expensive gadgets are hopelessly out of step with the industrial world of today. Their problems should be how to raise more money to buy more machinery and keep them running. It can make for happier and nobler people by providing them with all the luxuries and comforts. By means of machinery, the standard of living of the masses can be raised. No nation has ever yet been ruined by the use of too much machinery in a well-planned economy. However, I must stress here that this excludes machines used exclusively in the manufacture of weapons for the purpose of aggression or war.

CHAPTER 9

Let Them Wait For Their Money

I am sure you have often heard people say with an air of mingled wisdom and bravado: "Let them (creditors) wait for their money!" What a foolish thing to say! They are practically saying: "What do we care if our credit standing is no longer good? We don't give a fig one way or another and we don't think it will affect our business reputation either!"

This selfish and suicidal indifference to the rights of creditors has destroyed thousands of business people. Those who think and talk in such terms never get very far in the business world. They learn their lesson soon enough – when it is probably too late to do anything about it.

"I never pay until I am really bothered, or when legal action is threatened," they will tell you. These are people, otherwise intelligent, who make it a policy to delay payment of debts, who deliberately ignore monthly bills, and who pay up only when they are threatened by a lawyer's letter. And the amazing thing about it is that they seem to believe that they benefit in some way by sticking to this policy. To get money out of them is like squeezing blood out of a stone.

Strange to say, it is a common form of dishonesty even among some respectable people. But I think it is time that this practice or policy be branded for what it really is – one of the meanest forms of dishonesty. For people to buy goods from someone on the understanding that they will pay for them within a stipulated time, and then to keep that person waiting for his money long after that stipulated period expires, is nothing but cheating that person of interest that could rightfully be his or hers if the money was invested elsewhere. It also makes it very difficult for him or her to continue in business with all that money tied up in customers' debts. Bad debts and overdue payments have wrecked many businesses.

Some companies make it a policy to delay settling debts for as long as possible even when they are in a position to pay them. They have the mistaken idea that they benefit in some way by treating their creditors this way. They deliberately ignore or overlook the fact that they acquire a bad reputation and that people who do business with them are prepared to wait for the right moment to retaliate in some way or other.

Every company that has been in business for three or more years becomes known by then either as a prompt, slow or non-payer of debts. What apparently is not fully appreciated is that the longer payment is delayed, the higher the interest rate will be.

Business people should play by the rules of credit and do nothing to weaken it. It is the foundation upon which business stands. Without it, we would be treating one another as rogues. All business would have to be done on a cash basis, which would be impracticable.

Slow-paying companies damage the structure of credit. They endanger banking and the whole process of buying and selling. They create risks. They add to the uncertainties of trade and commerce and destroy the mutual trust that enables people to transact with one another in confidence.

You will find a blacklist of non-payers in every part of the world. These are the outlaws in the world of business. They are the modern bandits who abuse the system of credit that has been steadily built up by honest people.

To buy something and not pay for it is not buying. If it is done deliberately, it is theft. If it is not done deliberately, it will lead to bankruptcy. In both cases, money has been taken away from trustful people. In the first nine months of 1991, some 34,000 businesses in Britain went bankrupt. That works out to about 940 businesses a week, compared to some 550 a week for the whole of 1990. These figures were taken from The International magazine.

I would venture that a high percentage of the businesses that failed would fall into the category of non-payers. If anything, this adds enormously to the cost and risk of doing business. Much of it could be prevented if we had a keener sense of the sacred obligation of paying debts.

Even the world's nations can be classified as good, slow or non-payers of debts. It would be virtually impossible for some of them to service their massive debts. As it is, they find it very difficult to even maintain payment of **interest** on those loans they contracted so easily but found so hard to settle.

Another aspect of debts has to do with the recent extension of credit to the man in the street in the form of various credit cards issued by banks, finance companies and other consumer-orientated organisations. In fact, the proliferation of such credit cards and other electronic devices are rapidly transforming some countries into cashless societies. The danger of spending more than you earn is always there for those who make it a point to use cards instead of cash. This is because most people are apt to give little thought to something they don't see – money changing hands physically.

They don't feel the pinch until banks and financial organisations send them notices informing them that they have over-extended their credit facilities with them. Fortunately, governments are aware of the dangers of unlimited credit being extended through the use of credit cards. So they introduce legislation to limit the amount of credit based on the earning capacity of card-holders. Even then, these credit organisations go to great lengths to soften the blow on their regular clients because of the tremendous competition in this very lucrative world-wide credit card industry.

Then there is buying goods and services on "time" or what we more commonly call "instalments". Most people, especially those in the middle, lower middle and lower income groups, buy things on instalments. Of course, they pay more in the form of interest for the privilege of paying for the goods over a period of time. Those who want more than what they can pay for in cash must always pay a higher price.

The instalment system creates debt too easily. There is always the temptation for people to buy more than they really need, consequently making it difficult, if not impossible, for them to meet their financial obligations, even in instalments. A buyer's instalment obligations should never exceed 50 percent of his regular income. Payments should not outrun the value of the purchased article.

Retail outlets seldom, if ever, demand any collateral from their customers before allowing them to buy goods on credit. They are aware of the risks they are taking, but probably argue that if they don't do it, others will be prepared to do it anyway to drum up business. How much money retailers lose a year because some of their credit customers decide to delay payment or not pay at all will probably never be known.

There are a lot of people who grudgingly pay their debts only when they are forced to do so. These people must be made to realise how important it is to repay debts or the interest on them promptly if they want to maintain their credit standing. This cannot be repeated often enough, and it is a problem that can, and should, be solved through education.

When it comes to companies, however, it has generally been accepted that they need money in order to make money; and it is common business practice to borrow money in order to do so. To do this, they must establish credit, and inevitably they will now and then borrow money on the strength of their credit standing to finance projects to expand and boost business. So the finances of companies are usually in a continuous state of flux. They are invariably in debt, but it would otherwise be difficult for them to do business in the world today.

There is one big difference. Most companies are keenly aware of the dangers of defaulting in paying their debts or refusing to do so. While their money is kept rolling, they make sure that their loans and debts are serviced promptly and regularly, unless they are really hard put to do so. Then they will come to some kind of mutually acceptable arrangement on how best to solve the problem of repayment.

The best and, perhaps, the quickest way to establish credit is to save. First put money in the bank. Then acquire securities like bonds, stocks and shares. Borrow money on the strength of those securities, and then repay the loan promptly – this is the only way to establish good credit. Eventually, people can establish such a good credit standing that they will be able to borrow without offering any security in return. This is the ultimate in establishing credit.

Those who try to dodge the first step by buying things through the instalment system will pay a high price for their weakness.

No matter how small people's wages or salaries are, they should be able to save a little of it. If they cannot save, there is little hope for them – not in this world, at any rate. Saving means self-control. It means having a purpose. It means mastering your circumstances and beginning to move forward.

My own policy has always been to take every cash discount and to pay every bill within 30 days. I have never gone into debt for any reason. I have paid cash all my life, with only one exception. I have always maintained a large cash reserve, which enables me to buy things at the lowest possible prices. I have never paid a penny of interest in my life, and I have never used any other person's money. I find that it is much more profitable to use my own.

This is a simple and primitive policy. If it were generally adopted, it would probably put the banks out of business. I am not mentioning it in any advisory way, but I have found it a policy that enables people to make the best use of their buying power and to sleep peacefully every night.

But if you must borrow, be an efficient and honest borrower. Obey the rules of borrowing. Acquire a reputation that will enable you to borrow more and at lower rates of interest. Pay back money when it is due and keep your name or the name of your business out of any blacklist.

Borrowing has now been made easy by the extension of credit facilities. It is easy to buy with other people's money and then to cry "Shylock" when the money has to be paid back. Those who want something for nothing have no right either to buy on credit or borrow.

Underneath it all lies the question – how can people create credit and goodwill and get the most value for what they have to pay? Obviously, the worst possible way to answer this question is to say: "Let them wait for their money!"

CHAPTER 10

The Public Expects Too Much

There are probably lots of tradespeople who sit in their empty shops or stores and sagely say to themselves: "The public expects too much." They make the big mistake in believing that they are in no way dependent, as caterers, on the whims and fancies of other people for their livelihood. By some strange accident, they are in business. Such people have no business doing business. They should take on some other type of work, preferably jobs requiring very little or no interaction with other people.

People in business who put the blame on the public for their shortcomings are slackers. They are lazy and try to hide it by shifting the blame elsewhere. It is the patronage of the general public that makes work for them, and they have the gall to regard such work as trouble. They think that if only the public were not so particular and hard to please, they could be left in peace to sit in a comfortable chair and smoke their pipes or read a book. And so they talk themselves closer to liquidation.

To begin with, they have the wrong attitude towards business. No customers who go to their shops once will want to visit them again. They repel people, and create a feeling of dislike in those who drop in for the first time.

What is business if it is not doing your best to please your customers and in the process boost sales? Doesn't success in a business come always as a result of customers who are well satisfied with you and the products or services you sell? If then, people in business still firmly believe that customers expect too much from them in order to be satisfied, how can they possibly expect to succeed in their businesses?

Suppose a farmer said: "My soil expects too much from me. I will not waste my time in fertilising it." What could be more absurd? Yet this is the attitude of many shopkeepers and manufacturers.

The churlishness of many tradespeople is almost beyond belief. I once knew an ironmonger whose habit it was, when asked for an article, to place it on the counter, say gruffly how much it cost, then add aggressively: "Take it or leave it." Naturally, his business didn't last long.

Many shop assistants display a spirit of hostility to customers when selling goods to them. The same goes for many ticket-sellers at railway stations, cinema theatres and other places of entertainment. They are curt and antagonistic. Plainly, they regard selling as a bother, and they don't want to be bothered.

Some tradespeople go further – and this is not funny. They palm off defective goods on their customers by hiding the defects in one way or another. They are quite prepared to "kill" a customer to make a little extra money. Sadly, what is even more despicable is that they regard this as a "clever" deception.

Long ago, business was a battle of wits in the bazaars of the East. Some of it probably still exists. The seller puts his price as high as he dares and the buyer will start at his lowest bid. The haggling begins – each one trying to outwit the other – and this may go on for quite some time. Every sale is a contest.

This primitive idea has now been abolished in all well-managed, modern shops. There are fixed prices marked clearly on each item. And if there is a sale, each item is marked up with both the usual price and the sale price. There is no contest. The whole shop is run to please and serve customers.

We have learned that the Law of Retaliation applies to the business world. If we try to punish the public, the public will punish us. If we flout the public, the public will ostracise us and we will find ourselves left without a market.

Sooner or later all people, whether or not in business, run up against this Law of Retaliation. When I was a youngster, I once threw a handful of gravel at another boy who was bigger than I was. He picked up a large stone and threw it at me. The stone struck me on the head and I fell to the ground. That was a long time ago, but I still carry the scar of that blow. It marked me for life. That was my first lesson on the Law of Retaliation.

Most of us carry scars on our bodies and in our hearts as well, reminding us that it is not wise to antagonise or make war on others without rhyme or reason. By the time a boy or girl is 12 years old, he or she has usually learned this first great moral lesson of life – "If I hurt others, others will hurt me." Some never learn this lesson. The worst of them become criminals, and the prisons are full of men and women who persist in ignoring it.

Some people, early in their lives, discover another great law – the Law of Reciprocity. They find that if they help other people, other people will help them. This is the beginning of wisdom, happiness and success.

Reciprocity! It can be put in several ways. Basically, it means that you will receive what you dish out or reap what you sow. If you sow mistrust, lies and underhandedness in your business dealings with others, you can expect a dose of the same in return. It is a form of moral and social behaviour. Possibly behind every great business success you will find somebody who puts this law into practice.

To give people a little more than they expect is not philanthropy. It is the shrewdest of business policies. Do something extra. Surprise people pleasantly in some way. Do all the usual things, then do something unusual, something beyond the ordinary, to please your customers.

What every customer wants is personal attention. Formal civility and courtesy are not enough. The letter that begins – "Dear Sir or Madam," does more harm than good. People do not like to be treated like things nor like mere units of the market.

Why are doctors generally well-liked? Some so well that people won't go to any other when they are ill. This is because they give personal attention. They inquire about symptoms. They treat patients as friends. Everything they do is personal; their "bedside manner" is excellent. Some people who are not sick will even go to a doctor because they love the sympathetic personal attention given to them.

Some modern businesses, in their desire to be super-efficient, either frown or put a ban on too much conversation in the office. If you ask a question, you receive a short, sharp answer. Some organisations are run like factories. They treat customers or clients as though they are raw materials that must be speeded on their way.

This is a mistake. Almost everyone loves to talk – to converse, to communicate, to keep in touch, to establish some sort of relationship. Best of all, they like to be asked questions about themselves. People perform best when things are open and informal.

Most customers like to be called by their names – even by their first or Christian names. Everyone likes to be recognised. The peak of salesmanship is reached when a shop assistant says: "Good morning, Mrs. Smith (or Julie, if he is very familiar with her). We have not seen you for a couple of weeks. I have been keeping a brown leather bag for you – the kind you were asking about. Here it is." That is personal attention that customers find irresistible.

Friendship should be a business-building force. Unfortunately, in these days when profit is the only thing that matters, there are many sour-faced tradespeople who have no time to be friendly, polite or courteous. Their main concern is how much they can grossly overcharge their customers, especially tourists.

The fast life-styles in the shopping meccas of the world, where time is money, leaves little or no time for social graces. No shop or factory is so large that it can afford to neglect friendship. The reason why so many small businesses continue to prosper is that they provide the personal touch, and pay more attention to the importance of friendship than the big organisations do.

The concept now is towards large self-contained shopping centres or malls, boasting department stores, restaurants, theatres, banks, post offices, car agencies, concert and exhibition halls and shops retailing in all manner of goods. They provide a whole host of services.

It is at these centres and malls that courtesy and service with that personal touch should thrive. And you will inevitably find that these places survive and draw the shoppers because some merchants at these places, to their credit, have become well-known for their courtesy and personal service. They are leading role models for others.

There is a well-known saying: "The customer is always right." How true! Past successes, using that phrase as a yardstick, have proven that it pays to be fanatical on this matter of pleasing the public.

What has been of great help to top management in making wise decisions about what the public wants is the development of market research. It has now become the most valuable and indispensable scientific tool in the business world today to assess anything connected with a business – from consumer demands to business trends.

Manufacturers or merchants who know their customers best – who have studied their wishes and opinions – will sell more goods than those who merely follow their own opinions. It is now accepted that the goodwill of the public is the most valuable of all assets. Everything about the psychology of the buying public is learned. Above all, everything must be done to maintain the loyalty of customers if businesses are to grow.

The more we advance in our efforts to please customers, the more profitable it will be for us. "Love thy customer as thy self," is obviously a more apt and practical saying that people in business should take heed of than "The public expects too much."

CHAPTER 11

There's No Sentiment In Business

Now we come to the hard-faced employers, roundly disliked by their employees, who fume at the decline of their trade and say: "There's no sentiment in business." Their philosophy is: "Everyone for himself and let the devil take the hindmost."

These shortsighted fools do not realise that they are on their way to be the hindmost and that the devil will make them pay dearly for their folly. They can hardly call themselves business people if their sole motive is to make as much money as they can for its own sake and "let the devil take the hindmost". They have the lowest and stupidest conception of what business is.

But not all people in business are like them. And it is not true that all they are after is money. Money to them is simply a means of enabling them to live the way they want to. Money means the ability to get things done. There are few misers in the business world. And they are not typical business people either, because those who hoard money seldom become successful in business or become very rich.

They do not know that to make money, you must spend money. They do not know that every business is based as much on feelings and opinions as on facts and figures.

The "business face" is usually featured in cartoons as hard, unsmiling, emotionless. This is a silly caricature. It is also untrue to say that people in business are robots. They do not organise a company as though it were a regiment of tin soldiers.

They know that regimentation must not be carried too far so as to stifle or destroy initiative and good fellowship.

It is always better to break or bend a rule than to break a heart. Ruthless business people may succeed for a time, but in the end they are pulled down by the enmity that they create. Some companies are ruled by discipline based on fear. And fear, of course, does not inspire loyalty. Where there is no loyalty and company feeling, the profit oozes away through a thousand leaks.

Some literary and artistic people look upon business as greed. They regard commercialism as a mere matter of making money. This is, of course, another foolish mistake. Business is not greed any more than sport is rowdyism.

No doubt some people look upon football as a very rude and rough game. Many sentimentalists regard hunters as people who glory in the destruction of life. The main thing in big-game hunting is the thrill of the danger, just as the main thing in sport is the thrill of the contest. Only those who love taking part in the risk can understand what it means.

It is the same in business. The main thing is not making money, but the building up of a great company. Business is a game – a sport – a rivalry. Those who go into it for money alone will never get very far. The more money-minded they are, the less they get.

Business is not based on selfishness, but on something that is useful and worthwhile. It is, perhaps, the highest form of co-operation that requires a great deal of teamwork to go one better than your competitors. The average person in business, I would have no hesitation in saying, is personally much more generous than the average poet, artist or professor.

A truly efficient company is one that has been humanised. In well-managed companies, you will always find the personal touch. Gold watches are presented for long, loyal service; the sick and disabled are cared for; the aged are not left destitute; the ambitious are encouraged; new employees are trained and the efficient are rewarded. There is justice and sympathy as well as discipline and system.

Few people in business are as harsh as they appear to be on the surface. The question may be asked: "Doesn't a banker have a heart?" Why not? There is no good reason why a banker should have the manners and temperament of a security guard or a director's intelligence to be good at his job. He can be careful without being highly suspicious of everything and everyone. He can be sympathetic without being credulous. He can be friendly without being off guard.

However, it is a pity that there are some bankers who acquire a manner of aloofness and suspicion. They "lock" themselves up as efficiently as they lock up their money. They give you an impression of latent hostility. They are negative and unresponsive. This could be attributed to the fact that bankers are entrusted with large amounts of other people's money. They shoulder a heavy responsibility indeed, possibly much heavier than most people in business.

Still, bankers need not act in such a manner – as though they were detectives on the verge of bringing some criminal to justice. If they could only learn to relax and be more friendly, they would be highly successful bankers.

You cannot mention banks without thinking of money. So while we are on this subject, I would briefly like to say something about that much-maligned phrase: "Money is the root of all evil." Money itself is, of course, not evil or a cruel force. It is no more evil or cruel than sunshine depending on how it is used. Some people are money-struck, just like some people who overexpose themselves to the sun get sunstroke. But money, like sunshine, is one of the most beneficial thing in the world.

Wise business people are aware that all people are ruled much more by sentiment than by either reason or self-interest. Well, almost all. They get sentimental about historical places, monuments, buildings, etc. Isn't London or Paris or New York or Tokyo or any other city in the world as much a place of sentiment as of money-making? Don't business people get sentimental about such places and the things in them apart from doing business and making money? Of course, they do.

So business need not destroy the finer nature of those who are engaged in it. None but the failures and those who know nothing about business have this opinion. Business is a ripening force. A little knowledge of business may be a dangerous thing, but a good knowledge brings out all the higher qualities of our minds and hearts.

Business people have their hopes and ideals. They have their likes and dislikes. They co-operate as well as compete. Their business life does not turn them away from the appreciation of home life, of music, art, flowers and sunsets. No one in business can afford to be feared and disliked. Public opinion is very nearly omnipotent. It can never be ignored, even by the most wealthy and influential people.

Similarly, those who cannot laugh at themselves will find it very hard to make others laugh. After all, laughter is a creative force. It can motivate, heal rifts, prevent friction, and radiate goodwill and optimism. So laughter has a great role to play in every aspect of business.

Sentiment in business? And laughter, too? A most emphatic Yes! We certainly need more and more of both to lift business to greater heights.

CHAPTER 12

It Can't Be Done

Of the 12 mistakes mentioned in this book, this is the most dangerous and destructive of them all – "It can't be done." It is the slogan of the pessimist who is afraid to try anything new. It has ruined many companies.

Anyone who persists in applying outdated, costly and unprofitable methods to accomplish something, because that is the way it has always been done, is like the person who says: "It can't be done." He wields past experience – "there is no other way" – like a tyrant to block progress. This primitive outlook kills initiative and stifles imagination. He is like a judge who says: "We have always done it this way. So why change it? – all because he is afraid to set a precedence.

Experience has its value in preventing rash action from being taken. But it has its dangers as well. Often, it anchors a company to old methods that have been proven to be unwise and unprofitable. However, there are elderly people who remain young at heart and who use both their imagination and experience. But in most cases, advancing years slow people down and make them disinclined to try out new plans and ideas.

There is nothing sacred in business methods, No one in business should say: "As it was in the beginning, is now and ever shall be." No one who inherits his father's business should follow so closely in his father's footsteps that he cannot envisage new, better and more modern developments taking shape under his nose.

Some people talk of businesses being "established" as though nothing more can or should be done about it. This is a delusion. Many people think that because their businesses are small they are safe. Nothing can be further than the truth. In these days of large multi-nationals and conglomerates, no firms, especially the smaller ones, are safe.

Every company must move with the times if it wants to survive. The companies that stand still in a constantly changing business world will be bowled over. They cannot be managed successfully by experience alone.

It requires no intelligence to say "No" to a new plan. It needs only inertia and laziness of mind. The easy way is always to do nothing; to take the line of least resistance. And the easy way seldom creates large dividends.

I am not in favour of a shallow optimism that says "Yes" to every new idea that looks good. Such ideas must be viewed with suspicion as well as open-mindedness. But when any new plan or project has been thought out carefully and proven to be desirable, a wise and prudent person will say: "I am not completely sure that it can be done, but I think it is worth a try."

Initiative is just as valuable in business as experience. I once knew a wealthy person who retained two lawyers. "One of them," he said, "tells me what the law is and the other one tells me what I can do."

In every efficient company, methods are used to develop initiative. In some places, rewards are offered for suggestions and managers who can make the most improvements receive bonuses. Initiative means having the resourcefulness and energy to do something original without prompting from others. It is an entirely different thing from experience and just as valuable.

Many people who have become successful are afraid to make mistakes. They want to create a reputation of omniscience. As a consequence of this, they slow down and allow their competitors to forge ahead of them.

Wise people know the educational value of making mistakes. They know very well that mistakes can be used as stepping-stones to success. They make it a point to learn from their mistakes. Many of the most able business-builders made mistakes during their careers, but went on to profit enormously from them.

Were not new trades built up by research and experiment – by finding out how to do things that were previously regarded as impossible? Are there no creative thinkers – inventors and chemists – whose job it is to venture into the unknown and do things that have never been done before?

Large profits are not made by doing easy things. The profits in any line are divided among the competitors. If a company has no competitors, it will walk off with all the profits. That is why every efficient company seeks to secure a monopoly of their goods and services.

Novelties have a tremendous advertising value. Manufacturers and merchants are aware of the great attraction people have for novelties. It requires the agility and talent of more or less a showman to secure the favourable attention of the pleasure-loving public. The public needs to be attracted and entertained – to be given something they can talk about.

Many inventions that originated in Britain were eventually developed in the United States. Why? Because British capitalists said: "It can't be done." The United States has always been favourable to new ideas for several reasons. It was then, and still is, a relatively new country. There are not many traditions or universal manners and customs. It is made up of people of so many different nationalities and cultures. With such a hodge-podge of people, it was, and still is, easier to start a new business or to introduce new methods of doing things. Consequently, the United States has grown to become such a rich and powerful country because it is always prepared to be innovative – to put its money into anything that's new. Its people never say: "It can't be done."

Europe today can still learn from the Americans – that there are almost limitless possibilities to the development of trade and industry or, for that matter, in any other field of endeavour. What the United States has done, others can do too. Is it not true that many difficult things seem to be impossible at first glance until work on them actually begins? It is always hard to take that first step, but once taken, the other steps become easier to negotiate. You learn as you go along.

So that foolish word "impossible" is slowly but surely disappearing from the vocabulary of efficient people. "Impossible" only means that a thing has never been done. The impossibility of one generation becomes a commonplace fact in the next generation. Old people will invariably tell you that they have seen lots of so-called "impossible" things become realities. They will tell you that we are living today in an age of miracles.

Who would have thought at one time that we would be able to fly – and not just fly, but fly faster than the speed of sound? Or that we would walk on the moon? Or travel in space? Or put satellites in space that would enable us to see people in other countries live on television and talk to them? Or take close-up photographs of the planets Mars and Jupiter? No one would have thought so at the beginning of this century. "Downright impossible," they would have said. But these are commonplace things in our world today.

And they are only a few of the many wonderful "miracles" that have come about because efficient and far-sighted people refused to believe in the word "impossible". What would the Roman emperor Julius Caesar say about them if he were alive today? Would he not say that we have become as gods? Would he not say that the gods of Rome and Greece were mere puppets compared with the people of today?

Don't these modern miracles of science make the discoveries of antiquity appear as the clumsy efforts of children? Shouldn't the creation of all these wonders give us a new attitude of mind when we are tackling the problems of trade and industry or any other sphere of business? Should we not tackle all our difficulties and problems with renewed vigour, energy, courage and hope, when we look around and see all that has been accomplished?

What vast, new possibilities are now open to us! What a role we can play – we who have the privilege of being alive in this Golden Age of Science and Industry! We are now able to do more wonderful things than anyone ever dreamed of. With all this splendour of human achievement before them, how then can anybody in business, when faced with some difficulty, say: "It can't be done"?

Titles by Herbert N. Casson in the Business Success Series

How to Get and Use Money
How to Overcome Competition
How to Start and Build a Business
How to Win the Five Goodwills
The Managing Director Himself
Sell Successfully
Six Laws of Business Success
Twelve Tips on Finance
Twelve Tips on Leadership
Twelve Worst Mistakes in Business
Twenty Tips on Psychology
Window Display